Meet the
Fernan Friends

Written and illustrated by Tom Hagen
Published by Tom Hagen Photography
ISBN 978-0-578-77478-7

For Merald

The Fernan Friends are birds that live at Fernan Lake in the American Northwest.

The narrow lake has hills and trees on both sides and shallow areas at each end.

In warm weather, lily pads and wetlands grow at the shallow ends.

In winter, the lake freezes and snow covers the ground.

Let's go meet some of the birds that live at Fernan Lake!

Hi! I'm Hannah. I am a Great Blue Heron.

I live at Fernan Lake all year. It has everything I need to eat. There are so many fish and if the lake freezes I can eat bugs and other things on land. Since there is always plenty to eat, I never have to leave.

Howdy! My name is Oscar. I am an Osprey. I only eat fish. I live at Fernan Lake in spring, summer, and fall so I can catch a bunch of them.

When it gets cold, the lake can freeze and I can't get the fish. That is why I have to fly south for the winter.

Good Afternoon! I am Sonny the Song Sparrow. I live at Fernan Lake year-round.

In nice weather, there are tons of seeds and bugs for me to eat. If the lake freezes I can get food in the forest trees nearby.

Greetings! My name is Chelsee. I am a Black-capped Chickadee. I live at the lake all year. When it is warm the lake has all kinds of seeds and bugs to eat. In the winter I can find those things in the forest.

Hello! We are Mike and Mary Mallard. We are dabbling ducks and we get to live at the lake all year.

We skim the surface or dip just below to get seeds and plants in the water. In winter, we can eat plants and bugs on the shore.

What's up? I am Maury the Hooded Merganser. I am a diving duck. I dive in shallow water to eat plants and animals at the bottom.

When it's warm, there's a lot down there to eat. When the water freezes, I have to fly to a lake where I can dive.

Hey there! I am Kenny. I am an Eastern Kingbird. I eat flies, bees, and other flying insects.

The mild weather brings loads for me to eat. When it gets cold I have to find food in a warmer place to the south.

Hi! My name is Nick. I am a Northern Rough-winged Swallow.

I eat insects that fly above or swim on the lake. When the weather is good, there are lots of bugs to eat. When it gets cold, the bugs leave, so I have to leave, too.

Hello! I am Gladys. I'm a California Gull. I eat just about anything: fish, bugs, fruit, and even food from the trash!

I can live at the lake all year. There's plenty to eat when it's warm. When it gets cold, I can find food in parks, parking lots, or almost anywhere!

Birds can be anywhere you look. They can be in the city or in the country.

They can be on land, in the water, or in the sky. They can be in parks or parking lots.

They can even be in your own backyard. All they need is to know there is food.

So go outside and meet a new feathered friend.

We promise, you won't have to go far!

Bye-bye, for
now.

We hope to
see you
again soon!

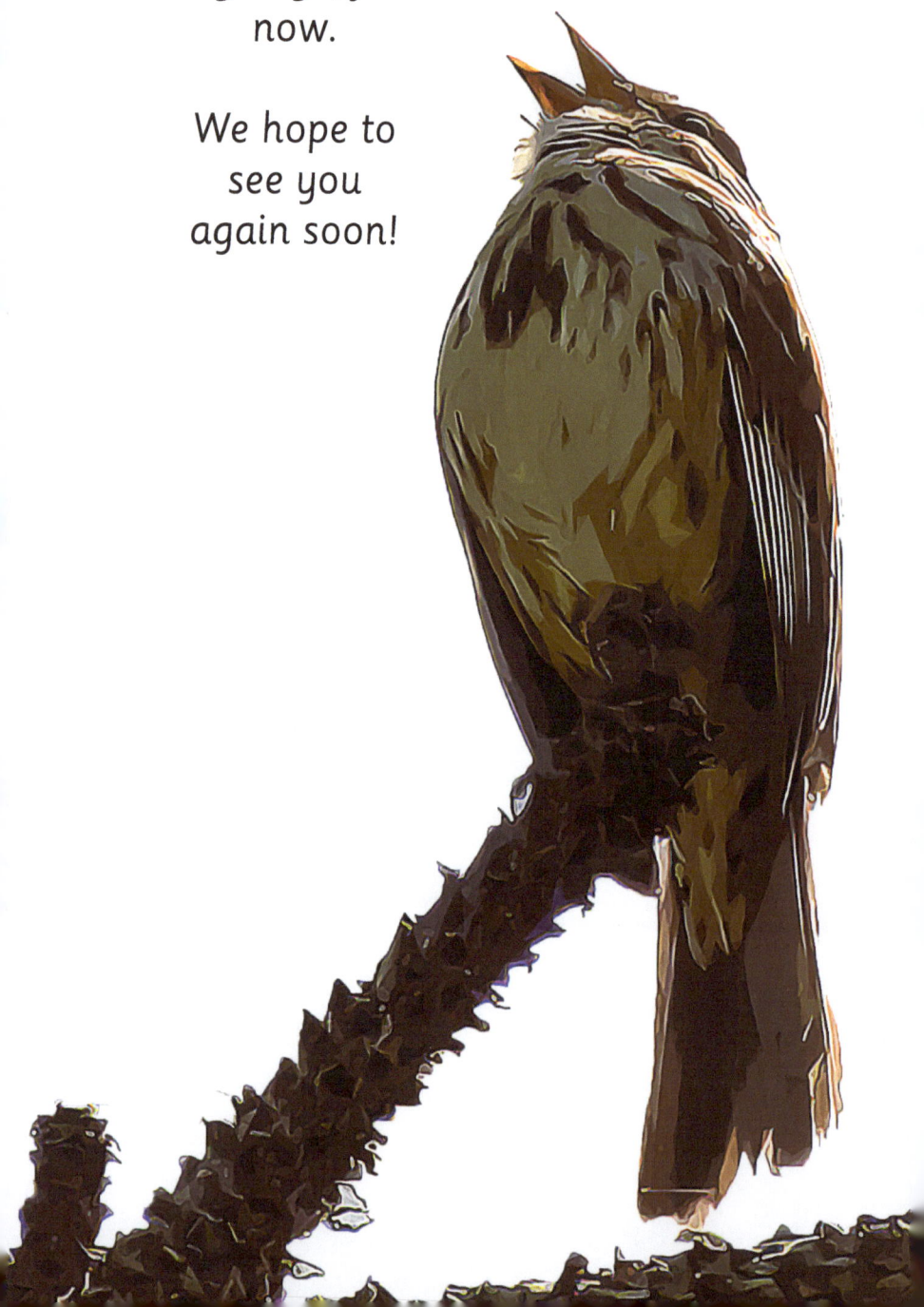

www.ingramcontent.com/pod-product-compliance
Lightning Source LLC
Chambersburg PA
CBHW041224270326
41933CB00001B/35